Nita Mehta's
More
Desserts

Nita Mehta

B.Sc. (Home Science), M.Sc. (Food and Nutrition), Gold Medalist

Wish You All The Best

NM-

SNAB
Publishers Pvt Ltd

Nita Mehta's

MORE DESSERTS

© Copyright 2002-2005 **SNAB** Publishers Pvt Ltd

3rd Print 2005
ISBN 81-7869-024-1

Food Styling and Photography: **SNAB**

Layout and laser typesetting :

National Information Technology Academy
3A/3, Asaf Ali Road
New Delhi-110002
☎ 23252948

Published by :

SNAB
Publishers Pvt. Ltd.
3A/3 Asaf Ali Road,
New Delhi - 110002
Tel: 23252948, 23250091
Telefax:91-11-23250091

Editorial and Marketing office:
E-159, Greater Kailash-II, N.Delhi-48
Fax: 91-11-29225218, 29229558
Tel: 91-11-29214011, 29218727, 29218574
E-Mail: nitamehta@email.com
 snab@snabindia.com
Website: http://www.nitamehta.com
Website: http://www.snabindia.com

Distributed by :

THE VARIETY BOOK DEPOT
A.V.G. Bhavan, M 3 Con Circus,
New Delhi - 110 001
Tel : 23417175, 23412567; Fax : 23415335
Email: varietybookdepot@rediffmail.com

Printed by :

BRIJBASI ART PRESS LTD.

Rs. 89/-

Introduction

This book is a dessert lover's dream come true! This unique book has been divided into various sections to give you a variety of mouth watering sweet recipes.

The first section is "Desserts From Around the World" which has recipes like *Grape Mousse* and *Yogurt Pineapple Torte* amongst many others.

The next is the Indian section. It has Indian favourites like *Shahi Tukri* but made the *low calorie* way! Here the heavy khoya has been substituted with paneer. Then the classics follow which include traditional recipes of *Chocolate Chip Pudding* and *Strawberry Cheese Cake*.

The Light and Fruity Desserts given at the end of the book has delicious recipes with pineapple, apple, oranges or watermelon too. So, go ahead and enjoy these sweet temptations.

Nita Mehta

Contents

Introduction   5

Desserts
From Around the World   9

Light & Fruity Desserts   89

Pineapple Yogurt Ice Cream   90

Baked Pineapple with Fruity
Caramel Sauce   92

Apple Meringue Pudding   94

Baked Caramelized Oranges   96

Glazed Pineapple Pudding   98

Ginger Fruit Salad   101

Mid Summer Desire   102

Desserts

FROM AROUND THE WORLD

Glazed Grape Mousse

Picture on cover   *Servings 8*

½ tin milk-maid (condensed milk)
250 gm black grapes (2 cups)
2 tbsp sugar
300 gm cream
4 tsp gelatine

GLAZE

1 tsp gelatine - soaked in ¼ cup water
½ cup black grapes
2 tbsp sugar
½ tsp cornflour - dissolved in 2 tbsp water

1. Cook grapes with 1¼ cups water and 2 tbsp sugar. Boil. Keep boiling
    on low heat for 10 minutes till syrupy. Remove from fire. Cool. Blend
    in a mixer for a few seconds till pulpy. Keep grape puree aside.

2. Mix gelatine in ½ cup water. Heat on slow fire till it dissolves.
3. Add gelatine to the grape puree.
4. Beat condensed milk in a pan till creamy. Add grape puree. Mix well.
5. Chill in the freezer till the mixture is slightly thick.
6. Whip 250 gms cream till slightly thick.
7. Beat the thickened grape mixture also till smooth.
8. Add whipped cream to grape mixture.
9. Transfer to a serving dish or individual cups. Keep in the fridge to set.
10. To prepare the glaze, soak 1 tsp gelatine in ¼ cup water. Cook ½ cup grapes with ¼ cup water and 2 tbsp sugar. Boil. Mash and cook till pulpy for about 3-5 minutes. Add ½ tsp cornflour dissolved in 2 tbsp water. Cook till thick and saucy. Add the gelatine and cook for 1 minute on low heat. Remove from fire and bring down to room temperature.
11. Pour the sauce over the mousse. Keep it in the refrigerator to set.
12. Whip 50 gm of cream till stiff. Pipe a star on the mousse. Top it with a grape.

Sicilian Orange Dessert

Serves 6

1½ cups orange juice, ready made
segments of 2 oranges - separated into small bits
3½ tsp gelatine
2 tbsp custard powder
½ cup sugar
1½ cups milk
1 big cup (200 ml) fresh cream - chilled
1 tsp orange essence
a few drops of orange colour

DECORATION
1 small dark chocolate - grated

1. Mix custard powder in ½ cup milk and keep aside.
2. Put the left over 1 cup milk in a heavy bottomed pan with sugar and keep on fire. Stir for a minute. Add the custard powder paste and stir till it comes to a boil. Simmer on low heat for 2 minutes till a custard of coating consistency is ready. Remove from fire and keep aside to cool.
3. Sprinkle gelatine over orange juice. When the gelatine gets spongy, keep on low heat to dissolve gelatine completely. Remove from fire.
4. Pour gelatine into the custard.
5. Add essence and 1-2 drops of orange colour. Mix well.
6. Beat chilled cream on ice to form soft peaks.
7. Add cream gently to the cooled custard.
8. Add most of the orange segments, keeping some for the top, and mix gently.
9. Transfer to a serving dish. Place in fridge for a few hours to set.
10. Decorate with some orange segments and grated chocolate. Keep in the fridge till the time of serving.

Chocolate Orange Gateau

Serves 6

QUICK CHOCOLATE SPONGE CAKE

2 large eggs
5 tbsp powdered sugar
3 tbsp maida, 3 tbsp cocoa
1 tsp baking powder
1 tsp vanilla essence

ORANGE TOPPING

1½ cups (250 gm) cream - chilled
1 cup orange (onjus) juice, 10 tbsp sugar
2 tsp orange rind (gently rub the orange with the peel on the grater to get rind)
2½ tbsp cornflour
4 tsp gelatine
fresh oranges - to garnish

1. To prepare the cake, sift maida, baking powder and cocoa. Keep aside.
2. Beat eggs, essence & sugar with an electric hand mixer till very frothy.
3. Sprinkle sifted maida mix on the beaten eggs and fold with a spoon. Pour in a greased loose bottomed tin of 9-10" diameter. Bake for 12 minutes in a preheated oven at 200°C/400°F. When the cake leaves the sides of the tin and is springy to touch, remove from the oven.
4. To prepare the orange topping, mix orange juice, sugar, rind and cornflour in a small pan. Cook till thick. Remove from fire.
5. Dissolve gelatine in ¼ cup water on low heat.
6. Add gelatine to orange juice mixture. Keep ¼ cup orange sauce aside.
7. Whip 200 gm cream till slightly thick, keeping aside 50 gm for decoration. Mix with the rest of the orange mix. Keep aside.
8. Soak cake with 2 tbsp of fresh orange juice.
9. Pour cream-orange mix on the cake. Whip 50 gm cream till thick and forms firm peaks. Pipe a border on the gateau with whipped cream.
10. Peel the orange and cut orange into round slices like flowers. Decorate with these orange flowers, slightly overlapping. Pour the orange sauce kept aside on the oranges. Refrigerate till set.

Creme Caramel

Picture on page 57   *Serves 6*

3 tea cups milk, 9 tsp sugar
3 tbsp milk powder, 1 tsp vanilla custard powder
3 eggs, 1 tsp vanilla essence
4 tsp sugar - to caramelize

DECORATION

100 gms cream - chilled, 1 tbsp powdered sugar
fresh fruits like goose berries or cherries or grapes

1. Mix the milk with sugar, milk powder and custard powder. Mix well to dissolve all the lumps. Keep it on fire and boil stirring continuously. After the boil, reduce heat and simmer for 5 minutes. Remove from heat and cool.
2. Beat eggs and essence well with an egg beater till light and fluffy.
3. Add the well beaten eggs to the cooled milk mixture. Keep aside.

4. Sprinkle 4 tsp of sugar at the bottom of a ring mould or a jelly mould. Place the mould over a slow flame holding it with a tongs and melt the sugar till the liquid turns golden brown. Remove from fire and spread it evenly over the base and sides of the mould. Cool till the sugar is set at the bottom and sides of the vessel.

5. Pour the milk-egg mixture in the mould. Cover well with aluminium foil and place a lid on top. Pour 1½ cups water in a pressure cooker. Place the covered mould in it. Pressure cook to give 4 whistles. Remove from heat. Let the pressure drop by itself.

6. Keep the pudding in the fridge so that it gets cold and sets well. Do not unmould till it turns cold.

7. To serve, run a knife all around the mould and then invert it on a plate. Give a slight jerk to the mould to take it out.

8. Whip the chilled cream with powdered sugar with an electric beater carefully till stiff peaks form. Transfer the cream to an icing bag and chill the bag with cream for 15-20 minutes. Decorate the pudding with whipped cream and fresh fruits.

Note: This can be baked in small individual ovenproof bowls at 200°C for 15 min. Cover bowls with foil before putting them in the oven.

Tiramisu

Picture on facing page　　　　*Serves 5-6*

400 gm (2 cups) fresh cream - chilled
1 kg milk - curdled to get paneer, juice of 1 lemon
1 tsp vanilla essence, 3/4 cup powder sugar
1 tbsp rum or brandy (optional)
2-3 tbsp cocoa to sprinkle

ESPRESSO COFFEE (½ CUP)

¼ cup water, ½ cup milk, 1 tsp coffee, 2 tsp sugar

OTHER INGREDIENTS

1 vanilla sponge cake - cut into fingers or 2 packs (15-20) choco chip biscuits

1. Boil milk. Add lemon juice to curdle milk. Strain the paneer. Grind paneer with ½ cup milk till absolutely smooth and becomes a creamy paste. It should not be grainy.

contd...

2. Whip the chilled cream with sugar, essence and brandy till thick.
3. Add the paneer paste. Now gently beat some more till firm peaks are formed. Do not over beat. If the cream starts looking granular, immediately stop beating. Put whipped cream and paneer mix in the freezer for a few minutes.
4. To prepare espresso coffee, boil water & milk together. Add sugar. Simmer for a minute. Remove from fire. Add coffee & mix well. Cool.
5. Arrange sponge fingers at the bottom of a small rectangular borosil dish. Sprinkle half of the prepared espresso coffee on the sponge to soak. If using choco chip biscuits, soak them in coffee for a second and then arrange in the dish.
6. Spread ½ of the whipped cream mixture. Level it gently.
7. Again put a layer of sponge cake and soak with coffee as above, or spread a layer of soaked biscuits.
8. Spread the remaining cream mixture. Chill in the freezer for 10 minutes.
9. Sift 2 tbsp cocoa through a strainer over the dessert. Decorate with fresh cherries and mint. Cover with a cling film and keep to chill for atleast 4-5 hours till well set. Cut into squares to serve.

Almond Souffle

Serves 8

ALMOND PRALINE
¼ cup sugar
½ cup almonds

SOUFFLE
3 eggs
2 cups milk
6 tbsp sugar
250 ml cream (1¼ cups cream) - lightly beaten
1 tbsp gelatine
1 tsp vanilla essence or few drops of almond essence

GARNISH
10-15 almond-toasted
2-3 digestive biscuits or good day biscuits

1. For the almond praline, put ¼ cup sugar in a small heavy bottomed pan and cook on low heat till sugar melts. Stir until sugar turns golden brown and melts. Remove from heat and stir in the almonds. Remove from fire and pour the mixture on a greased surface like a rolling board (chakla) to cool. As soon as the mixture cools and sets, crush coarsely to a granulated powder. Keep almond praline aside.
2. To prepare the souffle, sprinkle gelatine in ½ cup water in a small heavy bottomed pan. Stir on low heat till gelatine dissolves properly. Keep aside.
3. Separate eggs. Mix egg yolks, milk and sugar in a heavy bottomed pan and cook on very low flame (do not bring the mixture to a boil or it will curdle). Cook stirring continuously till a custard of a pouring consistency is formed. Remove from heat. Keep aside to cool.
4. When the custard is slightly cool, add the gelatine mixture (the gelatine should be of a pouring consistency, if it sets, warm gently again).
5. Put the vessel containing the custard mixture in a large vessel filled with ice cubes.

6. Stir continuously and when the mixture thickens slightly and is cold to touch, add the slightly beaten cream and essence.
7. Beat the egg whites till stiff. Fold the egg white into the custard mixture (the custard mixture should be thick but not set, if it starts setting remove from ice).
8. Fold in the powdered almond praline into the mixture. Pour in a serving dish and put to set in a refrigerator (do not place in a freezer compartment).
9. For decoration, place 10-15 almonds in a baking tray and roast under a grill in an oven till brown. Remove and crush with a rolling pin. Crush the digestive biscuits also. Sprinkle toasted almonds and biscuits at the time of serving.

Peach Trifle

Picture on cover   *Serves 10*

CHIFFON SPONGE CAKE

¼ cup flour (maida), ¼ cup cornflour, 1 tsp baking powder, a pinch of salt

4 eggs

½ cup powdered sugar, 1 tsp vanilla essence

THICK CUSTARD FILLING

2¼ cups milk, 6 tbsp vanilla custard powder

6 tbsp sugar, ½ cup finely chopped peaches, 1 tsp vanilla essence

TOPPING

1 tin peach halves, a few blanched almonds, cherries

a few chocolate thins (After 8 or any other chocolate) - cut into half diagonally

TO SOAK

½ cup syrup from the peach tin, 1 tbsp rum or brandy, optional

1. For the cake, sieve flour, cornflour, baking powder and salt.
2. Separate the eggs. Beat the egg whites till stiff. Add essence.

3. Add sugar to whites and whisk till thick and smooth. Add egg yolks.
4. Gently fold in the flour mixture into the eggs. Pour in a 8" greased and dusted cake tin. Bake in a preheated oven at 200°C/400°F/Gas mark 6 for 15 minutes.
5. For the custard filling, mix milk with sugar and custard powder in a heavy bottomed pan. Keep on fire, stirring continuously till it boils. Cook for about 5-7 minutes or till it turns very thick. Remove from fire and cool to room temperature. Add vanilla essence.
6. Cut the cake into 2 halves. Cool the cake to room temperature.
7. Place a piece of cake in a serving dish. Mix ½ cup peach syrup with brandy or rum if using. Soak cake with 4-5 tbsp of peach syrup.
8. Keeping aside 4-5 tbsp custard for the top, spread the rest of the custard on soaked piece of cake. Spread the chopped pieces of peaches.
9. Soak the second piece of cake too with peach syrup and invert it on the custard. Spread the remaining custard on top of the cake.
10. Cut each peach half into thin slices lengthwise to get thin long pieces. Arrange slices overlapping slightly to completely cover the top. Garnish with whipped cream, almonds and chocolates. Serve cold.

Date & Walnut Pie

Honey flavoured dates & walnuts are baked on a short crust pastry shell. A loose bottomed flan tin of 9" diameter is ideal for making it.

Serves 10

SHORT CRUST PASTRY

200 gms (2 cups) flour (maida), ¼ cup semolina (suji)
a pinch of baking powder
110 gms salted butter (cold and solid), 3 tbsp powder sugar
1-2 tbsp ice cold water to bind

FILLING

200 gm dates - deseeded and chopped finely
2 apples - peeled and grated, ½ cup water
4 tbsp lemon juice, 6 tbsp honey, 4 tbsp chopped walnuts

1. For the short crust pastry, cut cold butter into tiny cubes.
2. Sift flour with baking powder. In a blender put the flour and semolina.

Add the butter and churn for a few seconds. Scrape the sides with a spatula or a knife and churn again for a few seconds only. Do not churn the mixer too much. Transfer to a mixing bowl and mix lightly.

3. Add just enough ice cold water to form a dough. Wrap in a damp cloth and keep in the fridge for 15-20 minutes to get cold.

4. For the filling, mix all ingredients except walnuts. Heat on slow fire, for about 10 minutes, till pulpy and dry. Add walnuts, keeping aside a few for the topping. Remove from fire and keep aside.

5. To make the pie, roll out the pastry so that it is ¼" thick and 4" bigger in diameter than the flan tin or the pie dish, such that it covers the base & the sides of the tin or pie dish. If you find it difficult to roll it, place the dough in the tin and spread it out to cover the bottom and the sides.

6. Prick base with a fork. Bake at 200°C in a preheated oven for 16-18 minutes or till the pastry shell turns light brown. Remove from oven.

7. Arrange the dry filling over it. Level it. Sprinkle some walnuts on top if you like. Keep aside till serving time. At the time of serving, bake for 10-12 minutes in a preheated oven at 150°C. Serve hot with vanilla ice cream or fresh cream.

Cold Lemon Souffle

A delicious dessert for a summer dinner. So refreshingly different!

Picture on facing page   *Serves 8*

400 gm (2 big cups) cream
3 lemons (6 tbsp lemon juice)
4 large eggs
a few drops of lemon yellow colour
1 cup (150 gm) powdered sugar
½ tsp vanilla essence
4 tsp gelatine, ¼ cup water

DECORATION

a few glace cherries, lemon twists, 10-12 almonds - crushed roughly

1. Prepare a souffle dish by tying around it a double band of aluminium foil with its fold at the bottom so that it stands about 2" above the top of the dish. If you wish you can secure the foil with cello tape instead of a thread.

2. Extract the juice of all lemons, keep aside.
3. Separate the egg yolk and white of the eggs.
4. Beat egg yolks in a steel bowl with the lemon juice and sugar.
5. Boil a large pan of water. Remove water from fire. Place the bowl of egg yolk-sugar mixture in hot water and beat with an egg beater or whisk until creamy. Remove from hot water and beat until cold. Keep aside.
6. Add gelatine to ¼ cup water kept in a small pan. Dissolve gelatine on low heat.
7. Add gelatine solution to the egg yolk mixture gradually and stir well. Allow it to set a little in the refrigerator. Do not let it become too stiff or set. (Make quite certain that the egg yolk-gelatine mixture has stiffened slightly only before adding the cream and egg whites. If it oversets, i.e. solidifies even a little, keep it over a pan of hot water and stir till it is semi-liquid again).
8. In the meanwhile whip cream with vanilla essence till it becomes thick and attains a soft peak stage. Keeping aside ¼ cup (50 gm) whipped cream for decoration, fold in rest of the whipped cream, into the semi-

liquid egg yolk mixture. Whip the left over ¼ cup cream till stiff peaks form and put in an icing bag. Keep it in the fridge and use it to decorate the souffle once it has set.

9. Beat egg whites with colour till stiff peaks are formed. Fold in stiffened egg whites.

10. Pour into the prepared souffle dish, leave until set; then gently remove the paper.

11. To decorate, gently stick the almonds on the sides above the dish. Whip the left over cream (¼ cup) till stiff peaks are formed and the peaks can hold their shape. Put the cream in an icing bag. Chill for 10 minutes and then decorate the souffle with whipped cream, lemon twists and glace cherries.

Baked Cheese Cake with Fruits & Vanilla Sauce

Picture on page 2   *Serves 6*

½ kg paneer (cottage cheese) - grated, 1 cup milk
4 eggs - separated
150 gm powdered sugar (1½ cups)
2 tbsp dark rum or brandy, optional, 2 tsp vanilla essence
¼ cup almonds - ground to a rough powder
4 tbsp kishmish - soaked in warm water and drained
2 tbsp maida (plain flour)

TO DECORATE

kiwi or any fresh seasonal fruit - cut into thin slices
some fresh or tinned cherries, an orange segment, some powdered sugar to dust

VANILLA SAUCE
½ cup milk, 1 tsp cornflour, 2 tsp sugar, ½ cup cream, 1 tsp vanilla essence

1. Preheat oven to 190°C. Grease and dust with flour, a 7" loose bottomed tin.
2. Grate paneer. Blend paneer with 1 cup milk in a mixer-grinder till very smooth.
3. Add egg yolks to the paneer in the blender, keeping the white of the egg aside. Churn to blend well.
4. Remove from blender to a big bowl. Add sugar and beat well with an electric hand egg beater till smooth.
5. Sprinkle flour on the kishmish and mix well. Keep aside.
6. To the paneer mixture, add rum or brandy, vanilla essence, ground almonds and kishmish along with the flour. Mix well with a beater.
7. In a clean dry bowl, beat egg whites till stiff peaks form. Gently fold in the stiff egg whites into the paneer.
8. Transfer the mixture to the prepared tin and bake in the preheated oven for 55-60 minutes until firm and golden. Check with a clean knife or a toothpick.

Contd...

9. When done, switch off the oven heat and leave cheesecake inside the oven to cool completely, then chill in refrigerator.

10. To serve, remove cheesecake from tin and top with thin slices of any seasonal fruit. Open an orange segment in the centre and top it with a cherry. Dust with icing sugar. Serve with vanilla sauce or with chocolate sauce.

11. To prepare the vanilla sauce, mix milk with cornflour and sugar. Keep on fire and stir till it turns thick and coats the spoon. Remove from fire and let it cool. Add essence and cream. Chill in the refrigerator in a small milk pot.

$\mathcal{L}$emon $\mathcal{C}$heese $\mathcal{C}$ake

Serves 4-5   *Picture on page 67*

250 gm (1¼ cups) fresh cream
½ tin (3/4 cup) condensed milk - cold
¼ cup lemon juice (juice of 4 lemons)
rind (peel) of 1 lemon
a pinch or a few drops yellow colour

BASE
1 packet (10) good day biscuits
4 tbsp (50 gm) butter - melted

1. Keep the cream in a bowl and chill for 10 minutes in the freezer.
2. To prepare the base, preheat oven to 180°C. Break good day biscuits into pieces and put in a polythene. Crush to a coarse powder with a rolling pin. Do not make them too fine. Put them in a bowl.
3. Melt butter and measure 4 tbsp melted butter. Add it to the biscuit crumbs. Mix well.

4. Spread crumbs in a small loose bottomed pie dish or a serving dish, (a small square borosil dish in fine). Press well. Bake at 180°C for 10 minutes. Remove from oven and cool.
5. While the base is being baked, wash & grate 1 lemon with the peel gently on the grater to get lemon rind. Do not apply pressure and see that the white pith beneath the lemon peel is not grated along with the yellow rind.
6. Take out ¼ cup lemon juice. Add the lemon rind to it.
7. Empty ½ tin of cold condensed milk (keep condensed milk in fridge) into a bowl. Add lemon juice and beat well. The condensed milk turns thick on whipping. Keep in the fridge.
8. Beat chilled cream in the chilled bowl with an electric egg beater (hand mixer) till soft peaks are formed. After **soft** peaks are ready, beat gently with a **spoon** till **firm** peaks are formed. Beat carefully in a cool place or over ice, taking care not to beat vigorously. The cream should remain smooth and not turn buttery or granular. Put about ½ cup cream in an icing bag for decoration and keep in the fridge.

9. Add half of the thickened condensed milk to the cream in the bowl. Fold condensed milk gently into the cream to mix well. Fold in the left over condensed milk too. Add enough colour to get a nice yellow colour.

10. Pour the cream mix over the cooled biscuit base in the dish. Keep in the fridge for at least 3 hours to chill. To serve, cut into wedges or squares.

Glazed Strawberry Gateau

Picture on facing page　　　　　*Serves 6-7*

1 ready made vanilla sponge cake of 6-7" diameter
250 gm (1 packet) strawberries
1 tbsp butter
4 tbsp sugar
2 tsp cornflour dissolved in ½ cup water
1 tbsp brandy or rum, optional
200 gm cream
3 tbsp powdered sugar
3/4 tsp vanilla essence
3-4 almonds - for decoration

1. Mix 4 tbsp water, 1 tbsp butter and 4 tbsp sugar in a nonstick pan. Stirring continuously, cook on low heat till sugar melts. Cook further for 2 minutes. Remove from fire. Immediately add strawberries to the hot syrup and stir gently for a few seconds till well coated and glazed. Keep aside.

2. Add cornflour dissolved in water to the left over syrup of the strawberries in the pan. Cook, stirring continuously till it boils. Simmer for 2 minutes. Add rum or brandy. Mix and remove from fire.

3. Beat the cream with powdered sugar and vanilla essence till stiff peaks are formed. Fill 2 heaped tbsp of cream for icing the border in an icing gun. Keep the left over cream and the icing gun in the fridge.

4. Remove the glazed strawberries to a plate with a slotted spoon, leaving the coloured syrup behind in the pan. Keep the glazed strawberries aside.

5. Cut the cake into half. Spoon 3 tbsp syrup from the pan on each piece of cake.

6. Spread 2-3 tbsp cream on each side of the cake and sandwich the two pieces together. Keep the remaining cream for the top.

7. Top the cake with the left over cream, leaving the sides plain without cream.

8. Make a border of cream with the icing gun.

9. Arrange glazed strawberries on the cream, choosing the big ones for the centre. Put more strawberries around to cover the top.

10. Decorate with almonds. Chill and serve.

Note: Use plums instead of strawberries. Use 250 gm fresh, firm plums (aloo bukharas), each cut into half and destoned. Glaze them in butter-sugar syrup as done for the strawberries. Arrange the glazed plums with the rounded side up on the iced cake.

Black Currant Cheese Cake

Serves 12

BASE
1½ packets (15) good day biscuits
4 tbsp fresh cream
a loose bottomed tin of 9" diameter

CHEESE CAKE
500 gm fresh cream
1 tea cup plus 1 tbsp powdered sugar
5 tbsp level cheese spread
½ cup black currant jam
5 tsp gelatine

TOPPING
2 tbsp black currant jam
1 tsp cornflour
a few black grapes

1. Crush biscuits to a coarse powder in a mixer. Do not make it very fine.
2. Add cream to biscuit crumbs and mix well. Press into a loose bottomed tin. Keep to chill while making the cheese cake.
3. Beat 500 gm chilled cream with powdered sugar till slightly thick. Do not over beat.
4. Add the cheese spread into the cream. Mix well. Let the cream mixture come to room temperature, since gelatine should not be added to very cold mixtures.
5. Sprinkle gelatine on ¼ cup water kept in a small pan. Wait for 2 minutes till gelatine becomes soft. Heat pan on low heat till gelatine dissolves. Keep aside.
6. Add the gelatine solution to the cream mixture (at room temp) in a thin stream, carefully mixing continuously with the other hand. Mix very well. Keep aside.
7. Beat ½ cup jam till smooth. Gently swirl it into the cream to get a marble effect. Pour the cream mixture on the biscuit crust. Refrigerate till set.

8. After it is set, run a knife all around the sides and gently push the bottom up to take out the cheese cake. Place on the serving platter.
9. For the topping, beat jam lightly. Dissolve cornflour in ¼ cup water and mix with the beaten jam. Stir for 1 minute on low heat and remove from fire. Keep aside to cool. After it cools put a thick round of jam, about 3" diameter in the center.
10. Arrange fresh fruits in a heap in the center. Make a border of halved grapes or kiwi or any other fruit available. Cover with a cling film and refrigerate. To serve, cut into wedges.

Quick Ice Cream Trifle

Serves 8

3-4 black forest pastries or coffee pastries or any other
1 tin mixed fruit or 2 cups chopped fresh fruits - stewed in 3/4 cup water and
½ cup sugar with a squeeze of lemon, ¼ tsp cinnamon powder
1 family pack (500 ml) vanilla ice cream
1-2 tbsp chocolate sauce to top, a few almonds - cut into thin long pieces

1. Cut the pastry into slices, reserving cherries for the top. Place them in a shallow serving dish covering the bottom of the dish. Spread cream of the pastries evenly all over with a spoon.
2. Soak pastries with 5 tbsp of mixed fruit syrupso that it becomes moist.
3. Spread the drained, canned or freshly stewed fruit on the pastries.
4. Sprinkle cinnamon powder on the fruits. Keep aside till serving time.
5. At serving time, top the fruit with scoops of ice cream.
6. Squeeze a few circles within circle, (like jalebis) of chocolate sauce on the ice cream. Decorate with some almonds and serve immediately.

Yogurt Pineapple Torte

Serves 8-10

3 cups (500 gm) thick yogurt - hung for ½ hour
250 gms (1½ cups) fresh cream
150 gms (1 cup) powdered sugar
4 tsp gelatine
1 tsp pineapple essence
a few drops of yellow colour
2-3 slices of tinned pineapple - finely shredded

CRUST

1½ packets (15) good day biscuits
3-4 tbsp cream

GARNISH

a few glace or fresh cherries, 4-6 almonds - crushed to tiny pieces
2 good day biscuits - crushed coarsely

1. To prepare the crust, break good day biscuits into pieces and put in a mixer. Do not make them too fine. Put them in a bowl. Add 3-4 tbsp cream to the biscuit crumbs just enough to bind. Mix well.
2. Spread crumbs in the loose bottomed tin. Press well with the back of a spoon till levelled. Keep in the fridge for ½ hour.
3. To prepare the torte, soak the gelatine in ¼ cup water for 5 minutes. Heat on very low flame to dissolve the gelatine. Keep aside.
4. Whip cream with sugar till slightly fluffy but still thin.
5. Whip curd till smooth. Mix the whipped cream to the curd. Add essence and colour. Add the gelatine. Add the shredded pineapple. Pour over the set biscuit. Keep the torte in the fridge for atleast 4-6 hours.
6. Remove from the tin, alongwith the bottom of the baking tin. Serve as it is on a flat serving platter. To decorate make a 1" border of crushed biscuits. Arrange pineapple pieces on it. Sprinkle some almonds in the centre and place a cherry.

INDIAN
Desserts

Chocolate Sandesh

Serves 10

1 kg milk, juice of 1 lemon
2 tbsp cocoa powder, 10 tbsp powdered sugar
¼ tsp chhoti illaichi (green cardamom) powder
a few almonds - cut into halves, for garnishing

1. Boil milk. Add lemon juice. Stir till it curdles. Add a little more lemon juice if it does not curdle properly. See that the green water (whey) separates. Strain the chhena through a muslin cloth. Dip the chhena tied in the cloth in ice cold water for 10 minutes. Hang for 15 minutes or more to drain out the whey (liquid). Squeeze liquid, if any.
2. Put chhena, cocoa, sugar and cardamom powder in a mixer and blend till smooth. Transfer to a heavy bottomed kadhai.
3. Cook for 3-4 minutes till the chhenna turns dry and becomes thick.
4. Grease tiny biscuit moulds. Put an almond half, white side (cut) down.
5. Fill with mixture and press well. Invert on to a serving plate. Keep covered in the fridge till serving time.

Kesari Seviyaan

Serves 3-4

1 cup bambino's seviyaan (vermicelli)
2 tbsp ghee
3-4 tbsp sugar
8-10 kismish
a few almonds - chopped
a few pistas - chopped
seeds of 2 chhoti illaichi (green cardamoms) - crushed
few strands kesar (saffron) - dissolved in ¼ cup warm milk
pinch orange colour

1. Heat ghee in a heavy bottomed kadhai. Add vermicelli and stir on medium heat for 3-4 minutes or till dark golden brown, but do not burn them.
2. Add 1 cup of water and bring to a boil. Lower heat and cover the kadhai. Cook till the seviyaan are soft and the water is absorbed. Check seviyaan, they should be really soft or they will harden when you add sugar.)
3. Add the kesar milk, cardamom seeds, kismish, almonds and a pinch of colour. Cook till dry.
4. Add the sugar and cook for 1-2 minutes on low heat.
5. Remove from heat and keep aside for 1-2 minutes for the seviyaan to absorb the sugar well. Serve hot garnished with pistas and almonds.

Shahi Lychee in Paneer Kheer

A very decorative & a delicious dessert with an Indian flavour. Assure your guests that the seed of the fruit has been removed and replaced with a blanched almond to enjoy the fruit comfortably.

Serves 8-10

20-25 large lychees
20-25 almonds - blanched (soaked in hot water and skin removed)
10 sheets of varak (silver sheets)
½ tin of milk maid (condensed milk) (¾ cup)
½ cup of milk
250 gm paneer - grated
¼ tsp kesar (saffron) - soaked in 1 tbsp rose water
300 gm cream - chilled nicely and whipped till it turns thick

GARNISH
a few rose petals
a few green pistas - sliced

1. Peel and carefully deseed the lychees, keeping the lychees whole.
2. Insert one almond in each lychee in place of the seed.
3. Open up a varak carefully. Place 2 lychees with the broad end (open end) downwards on the sheet leaving some space in-between the two lychees. Carefully lift the paper beneath the varak to coat the lychees with it. Do not touch the varak directly. Keep the shahi lychees covered in a plate and refrigerate.
4. Soak the saffron in rose water.
5. Whip the chilled cream (chill the cream before whipping) till slightly thick.
6. Beat ½ tin condensed milk, ½ cup milk and saffron along with the rose water in a pan till smooth.
7. Add the grated paneer and mix well.
8. Add cream to the condensed milk mixture to get a kheer like consistency of the mixture (thick pouring consistency). If you like it less sweet, add some more grated paneer.
9. Transfer to a shallow serving dish. Top the milk maid mixture with lychees. Garnish with rose petals and sliced pistas. Serve chilled.

$\mathcal{P}hirni$

Serves 6

3½ cups (700 gm) milk
1/3 cup sugar (slightly less than ½ cup) or to taste
4 almonds (badam) - shredded
5-6 green pista (pistachio) - shredded
2 small silver leaves-optional
¼ cup basmati rice or rice flour
2-3 chhoti illaichi (green cardamom) - powdered
1 drop kewra essence
or
1 tsp ruh kewra

1. Soak rice of good quality for about an hour and then grind very fine with 4 to 5 tablespoonfuls of cold water (rice flour may be used as a substitute).

   Dissolve the rice paste in some more milk and make it thin.
2. Mix the rice paste with the milk in a heavy bottomed pan. Cook on medium heat, stirring continuously, till the mixture is of creamy consistency.
3. Add sugar and cardamom powder and stir.
4. Simmer till it is fully dissolved and then boil 1 minute.
5. Remove from fire and add ruh kewra or the essence and half of the shredded almonds and pistachios.
6. Pour the mixture into 6 small glass bowls.
7. Chill. Decorate each dish with a silver leaf and a few shredded nuts.

Suji ka Halwa

semolina pudding

Serves 4

1 cup suji (semolina)
6 semi heaped tbsp of desi ghee or vanaspati
1 cup sugar
2 cups milk
2 cups water
4 chhoti illaichi (green cardamom) - skinned and crushed
1/8 tsp orange colour
8-10 kishmish (raisins)
1 tbsp pista - cut into thin long pieces
8-10 almonds - cut into thin long pieces
1 sliver leaf

Creme Caramel: Recipe on page 16 ➢

1. Mix milk, water, kishmish, crushed illaichi, orange colour and sugar.
2. Boil. Remove from fire.
3. Stir to dissolve the sugar. Keep aside.
4. Heat ghee in a karahi. Fry suji on low heat till it just changes its colour.
5. Add milk mixture, stirring continuously for 7-8 minutes till the halwa leaves the sides of the karahi.
6. Remove from fire.
7. Keep in a serving dish. Decorate with sliver leaf, shredded almonds and pista.
8. Serve hot.

Paneer Kulfi

Serves 15

1 kg (5 cups) full cream milk - at room temperature
½ cup sugar
75 gm paneer - grated finely
2 tbsp cornflour
seeds of 3-4 chhoti illaichi (green cardamom) - crushed
1 tbsp kishmish, 1 tbsp shredded almonds

1. Dissolve cornflour in ¼ cup milk.
2. Heat the rest of the milk with sugar. Boil and keep on fire for about 20 minutes, till reduced to half the quantity.
3. Add illaichi.
4. Add the cornflour paste to the boiling milk, stirring continuously.
5. Continue boiling, by lowering the flame, for about 2-3 minutes. Cool.
6. Add paneer, kishmish and almonds. Check sugar.
7. Fill in clean kulfi moulds and leave to set in the freezer for 6-8 hours or overnight.

Low Calorie Shahi Tukri

Indian bread pudding.

Picture on page 1

Serves 6

4 slices bread
2½ cups milk
1/3 cup sugar
5-6 chhoti illaichi (green cardamom) - skinned & crushed
a few strands of kesar (saffron) dissolved in 1 tbsp water
150 gm paneer - grated finely
4-5 almonds - cut into thin long pieces
4-5 pista (pistachio) - cut into thin long pieces
1 silver leaf
2 tbsp desi ghee

1. Remove the side crusts of bread. Cut each slice into 4 triangles.
2. Heat 1 tbsp ghee in a non stick pan. Add 8 pieces and cook on low heat till golden and crisp. Remove from pan. Add another tbsp of ghee and fry the remaining bread till golden brown. Keep aside.
3. Dip 4-5 fried slices in cold milk and remove immediately to a serving platter.
4. Heat the leftover milk with sugar and illaichi. Boil.
5. Cook this milk till it turns thick (10-15 minutes).
6. Add grated paneer and cook for 1-2 minutes till it looks like rabri. Remove from fire.
7. Cool the rabri to room temperature. Pour the cooled rabri over the toasts.
8. Decorate with silver leaf.
9. Sprinkle shredded almonds and pista. Dot with soaked kesar.
10. Serve warm or cold, according to the weather.

Kesari Mishti Dahi

saffron flavoured fruity curd

Serves 4-6

3 cups milk
1 tsp cornflour dissolved in ¼ cup milk
6-7 tsp sugar
2½ tsp fresh curd - for starter (jaag)
1 tsp kesar (saffron) - dissolved in 1 tbsp hot milk
8-10 grapes - cut into tiny pieces
or
segments of ½ orange - pieces peeled

1. Boil milk & sugar in a pan. Reduce flame.
2. Add cornflour paste, stirring continuously.
3. Rub the kesar strands to extract flavour. Add to the milk.
4. Keep milk boiling on medium flame to thicken, for 10 minutes, stirring frequently.
5. Remove milk from fire. Cool till luke warm.
6. Put 2½ tsp curd in a serving dish. Mix with a spoon. Add thickened milk which should be luke warm.
7. Pour the milk back into the empty pan.
8. Add tiny bits of fruit to the milk (optional) & then pour it back into the serving dish. Keep undisturbed in a warm place for 3-4 hours till set.
9. Chill in the fridge for 3-4 hours before serving. Serve chilled.

Gajar ka Halwa

carrot pudding

Serves 4

½ kg carrot - grated into long shreds
1 cup milk, ¼ cup sugar, 2-3 tbsp desi ghee
5-6 badam (almonds) - shredded
10-12 kishmish
3-4 chhoti illaichi (green cardamom) - powdered
100 gms khoya - grated

1. Boil milk in a clean karahi.
2. Add grated carrots and cook uncovered, stirring occasionally, till milk dries.
3. Add badam and kishmish. Stir for 1 minute.
4. Add sugar. Cook till the mixture turns dry again.
5. Add ghee and stir fry for 10 minutes on low flame.
6. Add grated khoya. Mix well. Serve hot.

Milk Cake Tukdi

Serves 4

1½ cups milk powder
1 cup malai (milk topping), ¼ cup sugar
¼ - ½ cup milk
varak (silver sheet), pistas - sliced, for decoration

1. Mix milk powder with malai in a pan. Add sugar.
2. Add enough milk so that all the ingredients blend well.
3. Transfer to a heavy bottomed kadhai. Keep on fire and stir continuously till dry, for about 15 minutes on low heat.
4. Cook further for 1-2 minutes, stirring all the time, till the mixture forms a clean ball and it no longer sticks to the kadhai.
5. Remove from fire and transfer to a small, shallow (1" high) square or rectangular dish. Stick varak and sprinkle pista. When set, cut into squares. Serve.

All time
CLASSICS

Lemon Cheese Cake: Recipe on page 35 ➤

Chocolate Chip Pudding

Serves 8

1 packet (100 gm) chocolate chip biscuits
some chocolate sauce (ready made)

VANILLA SPONGE CAKE

2 large eggs - separate yolk and white
5 tbsp powdered sugar
5 tbsp maida (plain flour)
1 tsp baking powder, 1 tsp vanilla essence

CUSTARD SAUCE

½ kg (2½ cups) milk
3 tbsp custard powder, 3 tbsp sugar
½ tsp vanilla essence

1. To prepare the cake, grease a loaf shaped cake tin. Sift maida with baking powder. Keep aside. In a clean, dry pan beat egg whites till stiff.

Add sugar gradually, beating after each addition. When all the sugar has been used, add the egg yolks. Fold in the maida with a wooden spoon, moving the spoon upwards and then downwards (fold) to mix in the maida. When the maida is well mixed, transfer to the greased tin and bake at 200°C for 12-15 minutes. Remove from the oven after 5 minutes. Cut into thin fingers and keep aside.

2. To prepare the custard, dissolve the custard powder in a little milk. Boil the rest of the milk and add the custard paste when the milk boils. Cook on low heat till it turns slightly thick. Add sugar and cook for a few minutes till sugar dissolves. Remove from fire. Add essence.

3. Break all biscuits roughly, each biscuit into 6-8 pieces, (small pieces).

4. To assemble the dessert, in a medium size serving dish arrange a layer of sponge fingers. Soak them with some hot custard.

5. Sprinkle half the biscuits on it, to cover.

6. Again arrange a layer of sponge fingers.

7. Pour custard to cover completely. Chill. Sprinkle remaining biscuits.

8. Squeeze some chocolate sauce in a design over it, may be continuous diagonal lines, or in circles. Serve chilled.

Queen Pudding

Serves 6

3 large eggs
6 heaped tbsp rusk crumbs
4 level tbsp sugar
1 tbsp desi ghee or margarine
1 level tsp baking powder
½ tsp vanilla essence
1 tbsp each of walnuts, almonds and cashews - broken into small pieces
1 tbsp kishmish (raisins), 4-5 glace cherries - cut into thin rings
a small piece of lemon peel - cut into tiny bits - optional
¾ cup hot milk

APPLE CUSTARD SAUCE
½ kg (2½ cups) milk
1 heaped tbsp custard powder, 3 tbsp sugar
½ apple - cut into small pieces

1. Grease a round baking tin of 6"-7" diameter. Arrange lemon peels, walnuts, almonds, cashews, raisins & cherries in the tin so that they cover the base of the baking tin. Keep the baking tin aside.
2. Beat egg whites in a dry pan till stiff. Mix in egg yolks and beat again.
3. Add crumbs, sugar, ghee, baking powder and vanilla essence. Beat well to get a mixture of a thick **pouring** consistency.
4. Pour the mixture gently in the arranged greased tin, over the dry fruits.
5. Bake in a preheated oven for 25-30 minutes at 200°C.
6. When baked, remove from the tin to a serving dish.
7. Immediately pour ¾ cup of hot boiling milk, all over the pudding, to make the pudding extra soft. Keep aside.
8. Prepare custard by dissolving custard powder in ½ cup of cold milk.
9. Heat 2 cups of milk with sugar. When it boils, add custard powder, stirring continuously. Add apple pieces. Cook for 2-3 minutes till it coats the spoon.
10. Serve the pudding cold in summers with chilled custard or at room temperature with very hot custard in winters.

Orange Cake with Orange Sauce

Serves 15

1¾ cups maida (plain flour)
1½ tsp baking powder
1 cup orange juice
1/3 cup oil
1¼ cups powdered sugar
2 eggs
¼ tsp dalchini (cinnamon) powder
4-6 almonds - cut into fine pieces
1-2 tbsp brown sugar

SYRUP
½ cup orange juice
3 tbsp honey
1 tbsp cornflour

1. To prepare the cake, sift maida with baking powder.
2. Beat eggs till stiff in a clean, dry pan.
3. Add sugar gradually and beat well till frothy.
4. Add oil, little at a time and keep beating.
5. Add orange juice and cinnamon powder.
6. Add ½ of the maida and mix gently. Add the left over maida too.
7. Transfer to a greased ring mould, (a jelly mould with a hole in the centre). Sprinkle brown sugar and almonds on top.
8. Bake at 180°C for 30-35 minutes. Bake till a knife inserted in it comes out clean. Cool and remove from dish. Keep aside.
9. Mix all ingredients of the syrup and cook till it attains a coating consistency.
10. Transfer the cake to a serving dish. Prick lightly. Pour the syrup over the cake. Serve.

Note: When you use ready made orange juice, 1 small pack of ready made orange juice (Tropicana) is enough for the cake and the sauce also. If you wish, you may make extra sauce and serve in a sauce boat along with the cake.

Devil's Chocolate Temptation

Picture on page 77   *Serves 8*

COCOA DEVIL'S CAKE

1 cup ordinary sugar, 1¼ cups powdered sugar
½ cup cocoa powder
1 cup curd
¾ cups (90 gm) oil
2 cups (200 gm) plain flour (maida)
2 large eggs
1 tsp soda-bi-carb, 1 tsp vanilla essence

TO SOAK

¼ cup cold milk, 1 tbsp sugar, 1 tsp rum or brandy (optional)

TRUFFLE TOPPING

½ cup icing sugar - sieved
¼ cup white butter
1 egg - beaten lightly, ¼ cup water
80 gm bitter chocolate (2 slabs of 40 gm each) - Nestle, Amul

CHOCOLATE CREAM FILLING
150 gm cream
3 tbsp powdered sugar
3 tbsp cocoa

1. Grease a 9-10" round tin. Preheat oven to 180°C.
2. To prepare the cake, mix 1 cup ordinary sugar, curd, vanilla essence and cocoa in a large pan. Beat well till sugar dissolves and is well blended. Keep aside.
3. Beat powdered sugar and eggs till frothy and double in volume.
4. Add oil to the eggs gradually, beating all the time.
5. Sift flour and soda-bi-carb together.
6. Add ½ the flour and ½ the beaten eggs to the cocoa mixture in the pan. Mix well. Add the left over flour and eggs and beat well till the mixture is smooth.
7. Bake in the prepared tin at 180°C for 1 hour. Remove from oven. Cool. Remove from tin. Cut into 2 pieces. Mix ¼ cup of cold milk with 1 tbsp sugar & 1 tsp rum or brandy. Soak each piece of cake with 3 tbsp of this milk. Keep aside to cool.

Contd...

8. To prepare the chocolate cream filling, dissolve cocoa in a little cream and mix it into the rest of the cream. Add powdered sugar and beat till soft peaks form. Fill some in a icing gun for decoration. Keep in the fridge for 10 minutes.

9. Spoon out a layer of this chocolate cream filling on one piece of cake, which has cooled down properly. Gently put the second piece of cake on it. Press very lightly. Keep aside.

10. To prepare the topping, heat ¼ cup water in small heavy bottomed pan with chocolate broken into small pieces in it. Cook stirring all the time on low heat till the chocolate dissolves completely. Add butter and stir. When butter melts, remove from heat and add the icing sugar. Mix till sugar dissolves. Add the beaten egg and immediately stir vigourously, otherwise strands will be made. Heat on low fire, stirring continuously till the icing gets a thick, smooth pouring consistency. Do not let it boil. Immediately pour over the sandwiched cake. Chill.

11. Decorate with chocolate and chocolate cream swirls with the icing gun.

Devil's Chocolate Temptation: Recipe on page 74 ➢

Eggless Chocolate Souffle

Picture on page 103   *Serves 4-5*

2 cups milk
5 tbsp sugar
40 gm (1 slab) plain chocolate
1 tbsp cornflour
3 tbsp cocoa powder
3/4 tsp coffee powder
3/4 cups (150 gm) cream - whipped till fluffy
2 tsp gelatine
½ tsp vanilla essence

1. Mix cocoa and cornflour in ¼ cup milk in a small bowl. Boil the rest of milk with sugar in a heavy bottomed pan. Add cocoa and cornflour paste to the boiling milk, stirring continuously. Add chocolate broken into pieces. Cook on low heat for 3-4 minutes till chocolate dissolves. Add coffee and remove from fire.
2. Put ¼ cup water in a small sauce pan. Add gelatine. Dissolve it on low heat.
3. Mix the gelatine solution with the chocolate custard. Chill in the freezer till a little thick, but not set. Beat the thick chocolate custard.
4. Beat cream and essence till slightly thick and fluffy. Add whipped cream to chocolate mixture. Mix gently. Transfer to a serving dish or pour in individual glasses. Refrigerate till set. Decorate with whipped cream and chocolate.

Strawberry Cheese Cake

Serves 8-10

2½ cups thick curd - hung for ½ hour
250 gm (1½ cups) fresh cream, 2 tbsp cheese spread, 7 tbsp powdered sugar
½ cup strawberry crush or fresh puree of strawberries
4 level tsp gelatine mixed in ¼ cup water
some strawberries or tinned cherries

BASE
a sponge cake, 4-5 tbsp strawberry crush or jam - beat well to make it smooth
2-3 tbsp cold milk

GARNISH
whipped cream
fresh strawberries or tinned cherries, a few almonds, mint leaves

1. Soak gelatine in ¼ cup water for 5 minutes. Heat on very low flame to dissolve the gelatine. Keep aside.

2. Beat cream with sugar till slightly fluffy but still thin.
3. Beat hung curd till smooth. Add cheese spread and whip till smooth.
4. Mix the whipped cream and curd mixture.
5. Add gelatine solution.
6. Add strawberry crush and mix well to get a bright pink colour. Check sugar, add more if required, depending on the sourness of the curd.
7. Chill in the freezer for 20 min, or till slightly thick, but do not let it set.
8. Meanwhile, cut a ½" thick slice from the bottom of the sponge cake. Cover the bottom of a loose bottomed flan tin, such as to cover the base. Press well.
9. Sprinkle some cold milk on the cake. Spread 3-4 tbsp crush or jam and keep in the fridge to chill.
10. When the curd-cream mixture becomes slightly thick, beat it till smooth and pour over the cake in the flan tin. Chill in the fridge for at least 4-6 hours, till well set. Serve garnished with whipped cream, fresh strawberries or cherries, mint leaves and almonds.

Note: Left over cake can be made into trifle pudding with some custard & fruits or a fruit gateau - a cake layered with whipped cream & fruits.

Mango-Choco Surprise

Serves 8

1 kg full cream milk & juice of 1 lemon - to make paneer
¾ cup milk - to whip paneer
2 tbsp cheese spread
1½ cups chopped mangoes (pulp from 1 big mango)
200 gm cream (vijaya cream or fresh cream)
¾ cup powdered sugar, 4 tsp gelatine

TOPPING

1 mango - peeled, scooped to make balls, cut the left over into small pieces
chocolate sauce (ready made)

1. Boil milk. When the boil comes, reduce heat and add lemon juice. Stir
    the milk on fire till the milk curdles and paneer is ready. If the liquid
    (whey) is not very clear, you may add a little extra lemon juice. As soon
    as the milk curdles properly, remove from fire and strain. Leave it in the

strainer for about 10 minutes for the water to drain out properly & to get a solid mass (paneer or chhena). Put chhena in a blender with ¾ cup milk & blend very well till very smooth. Keep aside in a big pan.

2. Blend mangoes with ¼ cup water in a mixer to get 1½ cups puree.
3. Whip cream with powdered sugar and cheese spread till fluffy and of a thick pouring consistency. (Can use vijaya cream in tetra packs too).
4. Add cream to the chhena mixture in the pan. Mix well and keep aside.
5. Put the mango puree in a small heavy bottomed pan. Add gelatine and mix well. Keep on low heat for 3-4 minutes, stirring, till gelatine dissolves. Keep on fire till no granules of the gelatine are visible.
6. Remove from fire and add it to the cream-chhena mixture. Mix immediately. Beat well to mix all ingredients well together.
7. Keeping aside the mango balls for decoration, add the chopped pieces of mango to the mango-chhena-cream mixture. Mix gently.
8. Pour the mixture in a serving dish and chill till set.
9. Arrange mango balls in the centre and keep in the refrigerator (not freezer) for 3-4 hours to set well.
10. At the time of serving, put some chilled chocolate sauce on top in swirls. Serve chilled.

Pear & Almond Pie

Picture on backcover   *Serves 8*

PASTRY

2 cups (150 gm) maida (plain flour)
1 tbsp powdered sugar
75 gm salted butter - chilled and cut into cubes
1 egg separated, 1-2 tbsp iced water

FILLING

500 - 600 gm - peeled, cored and cut into thin slices
½ cup water, ¼ cup sugar
1 tsp lemon juice
4 tbsp (50 gm) butter
125 gm powdered sugar (1½ cups)
2 eggs, 1 tsp vanilla essence
50 gm almonds - ground to a rough powder (¾ cup)
1 tbsp flour

1. For the pastry, churn the flour, sugar and chilled butter in a mixer-grinder until the mixture resembles bread crumbs. Do not keep the mixer running for too long at a stretch. Switch it off in between and push the flour down the mixer with a flat spatula.

2. Once the mixture turns crumbly, add the egg yolk and about 2 tbsp iced water in the mixer, and churn until the mixture just starts to bind. Remove the mixture from the mixer to a bowl.

3. Bring the dough together with your hands, form into a ball, Knead very lightly, without applying pressure. Wrap in plastic wrap, and keep for 30 minutes in the fridge to chill.

4. Roll out the chilled pastry and line the base and sides of 9" loose bottomed flan dish with pastry. If it is difficult to roll, spread it with your hands in the baking tin. Prick with a fork. Bake blind at 200°C for 15 minutes or until the pastry is very light golden. Remove from oven. Cool and brush the pastry with egg white to seal.

5. For the filling, boil water, sugar and lemon juice in a pan. Add pear and cook for 2 minutes till crisp-tender. Let them cool in the syrup.

Contd...

6. Beat the butter and the powdered sugar together till creamy. Add the eggs one at a time, beating well. Add essence.
7. Add the almonds and 1 tbsp flour and mix well.
8. Drain the pears and discard the syrup. Arrange pears, (keeping some for the top) over the base of the pastry and pour the almond mixture over them.
9. Arrange the left over pears over lapping slightly forming a border.
10. Sprinkle some ordinary sugar (1 tbsp) on the slices and then pour melted butter on them. Put whole almonds in the center.
11. Bake at 180°C for 30-40 minutes, or until mixture is set and golden brown on top.
12. Serve warm or at room temperature, cut into wedges with cream or ice cream or just by itself.

Fig Pudding with Butterscotch Sauce

Picture on page 2 Serves 6

250 gm dried figs (anjeer) - chopped roughly
250 ml water (1¼ cups)
1 tsp soda-bi-carb
180 gm maida (plain flour)
1 tsp baking powder
2 large eggs
60 gm butter
180 gm powdered sugar
1 tsp vanilla essence

BUTTERSCOTCH SAUCE

¾ cup brown sugar
200 ml cream
2 tbsp (30 gm) butter
1½ tsp cornflour

1. Preheat oven to190°C.
2. Place the figs, water & soda-bi-carb in a saucepan, and cook for about 20 minutes, mashing well, until the mixture turns jam like and pulpy.
3. Sift maida with baking powder.
4. Beat maida, eggs, butter and powdered sugar in a pan till smooth.
5. Add the fig mixture to the maida mix. Beat well till smooth and light.
6. Pour mixture into a greased ring mould (a mould with a hole in the centre) till it gets a little more than half full. Pour the rest of the batter if any, into individual ramekins or small moulds (small steel katoris will also do), and bake in the oven for 20-25 minutes at 190°C.
7. To make the sauce, combine all the ingredients in a saucepan, and stir over low heat until dissolved and turns slightly thick like a sauce. Remove from fire.
8. Take out the pudding on the serving platter. Prick lightly. Pour warm sauce over it and serve it with ice cream.

LIGHT & FRUITY

Desserts

Pineapple Yogurt Ice Cream

Hung curd is used instead of cream for preparing the ice cream. Remember to check the ice cream an hour before serving. A very hard frozen ice cream does not taste good and nor does a very soft ice cream. So remember to set the regulator of the fridge to set the ice cream right. Sometimes when I see that the ice cream is very hard, I leave it outside for 4-5 minutes before I serve.

Serves 10

5 tea cups full cream milk
6 tbsp skimmed milk powder
½ cup sugar
2 tsp gelatine, 3 tbsp water
½ kg (2½ cups) curd prepared from full milk
5 tbsp powdered sugar
few drops yellow colour
2 tsp pineapple essence, 1 tsp vanilla essence
1 pineapple slice (tinned) - cut into fine pieces, optional

1. Dissolve milk powder in ½ cup warm milk and keep aside.
2. Strain the milk powder paste into the left-over 4½ cups milk.
3. Add sugar. Boil milk, stirring occasionally.
4. Keep on medium flame for 25 minutes after the first boil. Adjust the flame so as to keep the milk boiling slowly all the time. Stir frequently to prevent the milk from boiling over.
5. In the meanwhile, dissolve gelatine in 2 tbsp water on low flame in a heavy bottomed pan and keep aside.
6. After the milk has been on fire for 25 minutes, add the gelatine solution to the milk, stirring continuously. Cook for 2-3 minutes more. Remove from fire. Cool. Cover well and freeze till firm.
7. When the milk has partially frozen, hang the curd in a muslin cloth for ½ hour. Squeeze gently to remove any excess liquid.
8. Beat hung curd with sugar and both the essences till smooth.
9. Beat frozen milk till fluffy. Mix the hung curd in it. Add colour. Mix.
10. Transfer to an ice cream box. Squeeze pineapple pieces well and sprinkle on the ice cream. Mix gently. Cover nicely with a cling wrap first and then with the lid of the box and freeze till firm.

Baked Pineapple with Fruity Caramel Sauce

Enjoy it by itself or topped with some ice cream.

Serves 5-6

1 fresh, ripe pineapple
1 tbsp salted butter (softened)
3 tbsp sugar

BLEND TOGETHER
1 large mango - peeled and chopped
1 banana
½" piece soft ginger - grated

OTHER INGREDIENTS
½ cup sugar - to caramelize
½ of a family pack of vanilla ice cream
10 almonds - cut into thin long pieces, for decoration

1. Peel the pineapple and cut into rings of ¼-½" thickness. Cut ring into 2 pieces and remove the hard core. Chop into 1" pieces. Heat 1 tbsp butter in a pan. Add pineapple and 2 tbsp sugar. Mix well for a few seconds only to coat them with butter. Remove from fire.
2. Place the buttered pineapple in a shallow oven-proof dish. Sprinkle 1 tbsp sugar over it. Heat oven to 175°C and place the pineapple in it and bake for 25-30 minutes. Remove from oven.
3. To prepare the sauce, place peeled and chopped mango, peeled banana and grated ginger in a blender and blend to a smooth puree. Keep aside. (The puree should be 1½ large cups).
4. For the sauce, heat a thick bottomed kadhai. Add ½ cup sugar. Stir on low heat till the sugar turns golden yellow in colour (like honey colour). Do not over cook or bring to a boil, it will make the sauce dark & bitter. Keeping the heat low, quickly add the pureed fruit and stir continuously for a few minutes till the puree blends well with caramel. Remove from heat.
5. Pour the fruity caramel sauce over the baked pineapples. Sprinkle almonds. Bake again at 175°C for 10-15 minutes. Remove. Serve warm or cold, topped with scoops of vanilla ice cream.

Apple Meringue Pudding

Serves 10

6 apples - peeled and sliced thinly
¾ teacup brown sugar
1 tbsp salted butter - melted
4-5 almonds - cut into thin long pieces

POWDER TOGETHER

3-4 laung (cloves)
½" stick dalchini (cinnamon)
¼ tsp grated jaiphal (nutmeg)

MERINGUE

2 egg whites, 1/8 tsp salt
½ cup powdered sugar
1 tbsp grated lemon rind (from 2 lemons, preferably green)
½ tsp vanilla essence

1. Place thinly sliced apples in a bowl.
2. Combine sugar, spices and melted butter in a small bowl.
3. Sprinkle sugar over the apples in the dish. Mix well.
4. Transfer to greased baking dish. Bake at 200°C for 20 minutes or until apples are tender.
5. Remove from the oven. Cool the pudding. Keep aside till serving time.
6. To prepare the meringue, beat egg whites with an electric egg beater until fluffy.
7. Add salt, essence and powdered sugar and beat more until stiff peaks form.
8. To get lemon rind, wash the lemons and grate them gently without grating the white pith beneath the peel. Fold the lemon rind into the beaten egg whites.
9. Spread meringue (egg whites) gently all over the apples. With a fork make small peaks in the meringue.
10. Sprinkle almonds.
11. Bake at 200°C for 10 minutes or until golden brown. Serve warm.

Baked Caramelized Oranges

Serves 6

3 firm oranges - peeled and cut into 3 pieces horizontally (about 3/4" thick slices)
½ cup sugar, ¼ cup water, 1 tsp butter
a few cherries or black grapes or glace cherries
fresh mint sprigs - dipped in cold water, to garnish

1. Peel oranges carefully, keeping them whole. Remove white fibres without disturbing the whole orange. Cut the orange horizontally, without the pieces falling apart, into 3/4" thick round slices, about 3 slices from a medium orange. Arrange in a round oven-proof dish. Remove seeds carefully from both sides of the piece with the help of a fork.

2. Place a cherry or a grape in the centre of each orange piece. Keep aside.

3. Put sugar and water in a heavy bottomed kadhai. Give one boil. Heat on low flame, stirring continuously, for about 3 minutes, till sugar dissolves and the syrup reaches one thread consistency, that is, it feels sticky and forms a single thread when touched between two fingers.
4. Add 1 tsp butter. Revome from fire.
5. Pour the hot caramelized sugar on the arranged oranges. Keep aside.
6. To serve, bake for about 8-10 minutes at 180°C. Garnish with fresh mint.

Glazed Pineapple Pudding

Serves 12

SPONGE CAKE

4 large eggs
85 gms (1 tea cup) maida (plain flour), 1 tsp level baking powder
115 gms (1 tea cup) powdered sugar
1 tsp vanilla essence, 1 tsp pineapple essence, 1½ tbsp hot boiling water

OTHER INGREDIENTS

a tin of fruit cocktail or soft fresh fruits - cut fruit into tiny pieces (1 cup)
4 tsp gelatine, 4 tbsp water
2 tea cups milk, 1 tea cup sugar
1 tea cup curd - beaten
juice of 1½ lemons
1 tsp pineapple essence, few drops yellow colour

GLAZE

¼ cup strawberry jam, ¼ cup water, 2 tsp gelatine

1. To prepare a sponge cake, separate white and yellow of eggs. Beat egg whites till stiff. Add sugar gradually (2 tbsp at a time) and keep beating till all sugar is used.
2. Add yolks. Mix well. Add both the essences. Add boiling water, half tbsp at a time and beat more. Beat till the mixture of eggs and sugar is thick and frothy and is three times in volume.
3. Sift maida with baking powder. Fold in maida gently, using a spoon (not a beater) adding half of it at a time. Put in a greased and dusted tin 8-9" diameter (a big cake tin) and bake for 30-35 minutes in a preheated oven at 180°C. Remove from tin after the cake cools. Keep the sponge cake aside.
4. Sprinkle gelatine over water in a small pan. Heat on low flame to dissolve it. Keep aside. Mix sugar & milk and heat slightly to dissolve sugar. Remove from fire. Add gelatine solution to milk, stirring continuously. Let it cool down.
5. After it cools, stir in whipped curd & lemon juice. Add essence and colour. Keep in the fridge.

6. Arrange the sponge cake in a serving platter or a full plate.
7. Soak with syrup of tinned fruit or with cold milk to make the cake moist. Touch with the hand to check that it feels moist. Spread fruits. Keep aside.
8. When the yogurt is slightly thick but not yet set, spoon over the fruits on the cake. Let it fall on the sides and cover the sides too. Chill in the freezer to set fast.
9. To prepare the glaze, dissolve gelatine in water. Keep on very low heat till it dissolves. Stir in the jam. Cook for 1-2 minutes on low heat. Remove from fire.
10. When the glaze is beginning to set, spoon it over the set yogurt. Arrange fruits on the glaze. Keep in the refrigerator and not in the freezer till serving time.

Ginger Fruit Salad with Ice cream

Serves 4

2 red apples - cut into small pieces without peeling
2 oranges, ½ cup green grapes, ½ cup black grapes
2 bananas - cut into round slices
½ cup gingerale
1 tbsp lemon juice
8-10 almonds, a few mint leaves - chopped
vanilla ice cream - to serve

1. Core and dice the apples but do not peel them.
2. Peel oranges and divide into segments, discarding all the white fibres.
3. Put all the fruits in a serving bowl and add the gingerale. Toss gently and leave in the refrigerator for 30 minutes for marination.
4. Drain fruit and put some fruit in a bowl or individual cups. Top with ice cream scoops. Again put the left over fruits.
5. Garnish with sliced almonds and mint leaves.

Ice Cream Watermelon Surprise

Picture on page 1   *Serves 8*

1 small (2 kg approx.) watermelon (tarbooz), 1 litre vanilla ice cream

SAUCE
3 cups watermelon puree, 1 tbsp cornflour, 1 tbsp butter
½ cup strawberry crush, 2 tbsp mixed nuts

1. Cut the watermelon, deseed it. Cut ¾ of the watermelon into neat ½" squares or make balls with a scoop. Freeze them in the freezer.
2. Puree the remaining watermelon in a blender to get about 3 cups.
3. For the sauce, mix cornflour in ½ cup puree and add to the rest of the puree. Cook on medium heat till thick. Remove from fire. Cool and add strawberry crush.
4. At the time of serving, spread ¼ of the sauce in a platter. Arrange scoops of ice cream on it. Fill the platter with frozen watermelon balls.
5. Pour the watermelon sauce over the ice cream scoops. Top with nuts. Garnish with mint leaves. Serve immediately.

Eggless Chocolate Souffle: Recipe on page 78 ⊳

Nita Mehta's BEST SELLERS (Vegetarian)

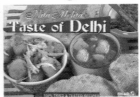
Taste of DELHI

NEW MICROWAVE

MEXICAN Vegetarian

Taste of PUNJAB

JHATPAT Khaana

CONTINENTAL Vegetarian

Eggless Desserts

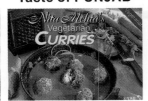
Vegetarian CURRIES

Eggless OVEN Recipes

Food for Children

Different ways with CHAAWAL

Different ways with VEGETABLES